819.1254 DON
Spirit engine /
Donlan, John.
771206

SPIRIT ENGINE

SPIRIT ENGINE

Poems

JOHN DONLAN

Brick Books

Library and Archives Canada Cataloguing in Publication

Donlan, John
    Spirit engine / John Donlan.

Poems.
ISBN 978-1-894078-63-4

    1. Nature—Poetry. I. Title.
PS8557.O536S65 2008   C811'.54   C2007-905651-2

We acknowledge the Canada Council for the Arts, the Government of
Canada through the Book Publishing Industry Development Program
(BPIDP), and the Ontario Arts Council for their support of our
publishing program.

The cover photograph is by Steve Reyes. KUHL & TIDWELL TOP
FUEL DRAGSTER DOING A FIRE BURNOUT AT ORANGE
COUNTY RACEWAY 1970. 3 gallons of gas, a match, and poof! All
paint burned off car, along with chute pack.

The author photograph was taken by Miriam Clavir.

The book is set in Minion Pro and Rotis Sans.

Design and layout by Alan Siu.

Printed and bound by Sunville Printco Inc.

Brick Books
431 Boler Road, Box 20081
London, Ontario N6K 4G6

www.brickbooks.ca

for Miriam

Contents

Stone Beach

Rock folded and refolded.

To Loss:
You poor boob, why don't you
get over it?

Bitter pleasure of not writing:
"Martha I'm mourning,
painting the sacred book black;"
"secret glee of withholding, inaction,
strong ribbed chest around a vacuum."

I don't have time for that foolishness.

I'm out of my zone, 27
heartbeats in 10 seconds,
scrambling up to the West Lion ridge.

Flathead six full out,
every millimetre packed with incident.

Thumbing and re-thumbing
this dog-eared book.

October 6, 1998

Bushed

for Stanley Knowles

1

Half in love is more than I expected,
deserved, really, given my dark destination.
How many more beats, my heart?
Do you know how much I love you?
Here's something decent people can enjoy.
Curtains of cold rain brush the rocky slopes.
Hurtin' music, the body's sad counter
to all that clever talk, those explanations
falling unheard as snow through yellow leaves.
Who needs to know how much a mountain weighs?
Sometimes the feel, the heaviness, of flesh
is more knowledge than you can bear.
You haul it like a suitcase, mind elsewhere,
so you don't spend your life saying goodbye,
goodbye, blood hum and aspen tremor singing
the simple, hopeless love of being here.
You're going, and you're coming back as rain,
as waterfall, as rock, as mountain flour,
wholly surrendered to the laws of downwardness
after a life contending. But not yet.
You're still pummelled by the chemistry of desire,
by the will's manic sheepdog chivvying
your attention towards the beauty of the world
as if to prove you're more than a witness,
you're implicated in these goings-on,
but mustn't worry. Repeat after me:

Bow Falls. Bow Falls. Bow Falls. Bow Falls. Bow Falls.

2

Near river water, blood almost remembers
long travels after and before this body,
being drawn through other lives and distilled
out into clouds, who claim to have forgotten us
and remain distant, even when we walk
among them in the rain forest, and breathe
their droplets in, and see them dew our clothes.

Griefs so strong they would outlive a lifetime
know only the extinction of the cells
of their prison frees them into unknowing.
We all want to be historyless
if that's not how we say it to ourselves;
nothing we say can touch the forest pond's
shining, wet edges, mare's tails,
water lilies, water hyacinths
building energy, black oozy shore.

If one time you lie where you have fallen,
half-dreaming your strength will drain away and down
to feed the world, you find the opposite:
you're like the giant who wrestled Hercules —
he drooped like an invalid, held in the air,
but, struck down to Earth, his mother, he came back stronger.
You inhale the smell of ground, the growing
grass, the moulds, the moss, invisible
creatures, spores, all living forms
keeping their selves, unfathomable richness.
You almost sense, under the pond's reflection,
your other nature, nature under all.

January 24, 1999

Soil Building

Sometimes you withdraw so far from the world
you mistrust even the surf of cherry bloom
crashing overhead — garish, unbelievable
happiness. What is there to say

after the finch's heart-piercing outburst?
A varied thrush gives a low, buzzing whistle.
A vee of Canada geese wavers north-west:
their thrilling cries pull each other up the coast.

Under the laurel, lily shoots barely visible
against sparrowy ground — the brown of an old photo's
deepest shadows: a battered board
kitchen couch where your father lies asleep.

A log house. Filthy towel, razor strop,
dipper and pail. A mirror darkening
coppery mica colour, its cheap backing
fracturing, flaking. Old injuries are over.

May 5, 1999

Columbine

for Stephen Reid

Cloudy wrecks pile up
along the coast,
Carrall and Hastings,
in Pigeon Park pink spindrift

of fallen blossom, browning petals
stick to boot treads of "poor
lost souls," veins daily
delivering the same bad news.

This June one crow child
can't get enough: it calls and calls
long after growing parent-sized. No one
knows what's the matter.

Leaving the mutter and ache
and fuss of self, your eye travels
the moon's path over the lake: unlimited room
for losses, above or below the gleaming water.

July 2, 1999

Across the Line

for Elizabeth MacCallum and John Fraser

You learn patience from white pine:
everything the wind wanted to say
confined to a few gestures. When the wind
insists, all the branches point one way.

You learn anarchy from grass: in its forest
of columns, all more or less the same height,
distinguishing individual stems in the green and gold
distance is wonderful training for the sight.

You learn protection from granite, a patron
of the art of ancient, delicate lichen: you walk
carefully, and when the white-throated sparrow
sings, "Dear, sweet, Canada Canada Canada,"

you don't talk. Seeing water beyond water,
you learn loss: you might never go there, and even here
there is more than you have time to love
in your brief life — look how deep, how clear!

July 8, 1999

Noise

for Ken Snyder

A tern scans the shallows,
feeding, hunting, figure-eighting the bay;
you envy her bedrock purity
of intent, wide-open awareness

for a few sprat, to keep a bird alive.
The city stuttering through your attention
is some excuse — these nihilistic kids
have it much harder — but what's the more

you expect of yourself? Nothing especially
human: in the spirit
of wolverines tracking the reek of death
over a mountain pass to the next valley;

weeds cozy in sidewalk cracks;
grimy spudgers scavenging Starbucks crumbs;
just so you forget
what you don't need.

November 19, 1999

Diary

Bloor's body a worn-out cat machine
under the rickety winter garden,
settling mound.
Too much history, "like a ball and chain."

While we remember how the pansy-faced
longhair dozed on the tea-cozy, sodden grey
scraps of coyote on the CN main line blur
to unreadable text.

We'd be extinct
without this gift for containing illuminated bits
of loved lives without also storing the growing dark
of their unending endings, but

evolution's over.
The various lovely creatures starve and die
and the future denies us many more slipping glimpses
of domestic or wild lives.

February 15, 2000

Bush Blues

(tuning: Vestapol)

My old neighbour made his own canoe
Man had the how, he carved his own canoe
Peeled off birch bark and sewed it like a shoe.

Try paddling now you're swamping in the wake
Big power boats, they swamp you in their wake
All that oil sure don't calm the lake.

Where's all the frogs that used to sing so sweet?
Every summer, sang this boy to sleep?
You can't find one green frog in all B.C.

Where's all the salmon, killer whales would eat?
Whales killing sea otters, orcas got to eat.
Whale can't open tins like you and me.

Last wolves in Banff Park, dying fast and slow
In four-lane traffic, dying fast and slow
You can't teach a wolf to cross the road.

Too many people, everyone says so
Too many people, everyone says so
Wish I never lived to see the wild things go.

Pink

Marvellous how the face
falls in, paling and fissuring,
blood slower to surface
and reveal its passionate truths

for which words are worse than useless.
It's all good: see those two trees
kissing in the wind like shy children
pushed together by their teasing friends?

That's your Grendel, your invader. You
call time an abstraction, and stare
at its bootprint on your face, your hair
"like a birch broom in a fit" — you're nature too,

though not, like nature, immortal. Above the belt
you're growing a "corporation," which could kill you.
So? — to a sharp knife
comes a tough steak.

May 25, 2000

Object

For some, drawing is pleasure; for you, paint
washes your heart out into the world.
Absorbed in a rectangle of coloured paper
you have become a part of the landscape

and cannot vanish. Night terrors
force us into our most compact container
against annihilation; they're the violent
inverse of this outward moving

but share its dreamy power
to waken us to what we didn't know
we were: you are that screaming child;
you are that fall of snow.

June 2, 2000

Gratitude

Is it gratitude you feel when a pine
(with leaves much paler than others, maybe diseased)
offers bursts of brilliant sulfur-orange
budding tips to the level sun?

.

Pleasure, certainly, at receiving
something desired, without labour
or expectation, though it wasn't intended
for you, an overheard conversation

when you're solitary and hungry for speech
and companionship. The tree never made
such beauty for you, nor the marten, who feels
who knows what, chasing through those colours:

still, you're grateful. You write your poem
from necessity, as the tree and the marten
live, and they're as much your audience
as anyone else you could name or speak to.

June 10, 2000

Prey

I'm designed for this: reptilian
robins cocked above buried insects
strike like pickaxes; warblers snatch
minute blue butterflies out of the air;

hunting's hardwired into me, love and need
united. What will I pursue
for the years left of my life?
Often I'm lost, the world falling

away in waste or shovelled into oblivion,
the hole in me unhealing. Desire in action
equals work: if I'm not the boss
at least it kills time. Remember

that first kill: it sickened me. Then
roadside pop bottles: I washed them
in the lake — two cents, and six equal
one pop. I'm still looking.

June 16, 2000

Fountain

How can you change your life? Like a wavering fountain's
column, it is continuously refreshed
from a reservoir deeper than sleep,
peopled with a dreamy observing self

and an impassioned cast of other selves whose dramas
can be the subject of interrogation, but only
if retrieved, like the pieces of a plane
that crashed into the sea.

This questioning, alone or guided, is the beginning
of change; perhaps it is the end; it is
endless. And, after all, the fountain plays
in the breeze and light of everyday

and lives in its air, freely offering up
itself, for others' solace, and to change
entirely: for what are clouds? — white water
flying, vanishing, becoming sky.

June 24, 2000

Here

for Jimmy Donlan, 1901-1982

Goodbye, heaven, goodbye, paradise.
Happiness doesn't need so much:
nothing bothering you, "some bush to look out on."
A loon drifts down the lake, asleep.

No young this summer: can it be grieving?
At home on the whole lake, only itself
to feed, it wakes, looks around, drifts.
This is too little, and too much, for some

who have to see themselves in every surface:
the shore, a swamp of desire, birth, and song
manicured, a carpet of bluegrass and ants;
do you think you'll get younger if you replace

that old campaigner you're married to?
You'd have to cover all the mirrors
to pretend there's some other way out of here.

July 11, 2000

Survivor

At the cottage, eh? — summer vacation
on the rocks. So many years of ice
have smoothed them beautiful as naked bodies
mostly underwater, the oldest forms

on earth, their age incomprehensible.
Our generations flicker past like shadows
of clouds, or webs of wave-light rippling
through shallows; greedy, desperate for time

whose molten flow seems locked
in the swirl of granite at our feet.
The elemental animal
has so much to relearn and to forget.

Close attention to the sky erases
history; the surface of the lake
calls endlessly to your body of water:
"Try to stay awake," and "Come on under."

July 21, 2000

Influence

for Elizabeth Bishop

Dear Inner Voice, "*bête comme un peintre,*"
all we ask of you is to mimic, limb and trunk,
love as well made as any limb and trunk,
while you call and recall our dearest loves,

those as yet unknown to us,
those lost to time,
one who warms up to us slowly
after a day at work leaves her rigid with crankiness

till she eventually laughs while she helps us make dinner; .
Inner Voice, help us speak
in the language of animals and plants, so we speak for more
than a species whose original sin or genetic stain

is to be too successful and make earth's heaven a hell:
so we sound as close to silence as wind in grass,
as steady as a cricket who counts the heat of the day,
selfless as a bird no one will ever hear.

September 18, 2000

Lo

Refusing the cozy comradeship of injury
the great big sea looks out and away
from the oil-numbed surf nudging its blackened corpses.
A tiny tanker edges towards the sky.

"I have a higher calling," says the sea.
"I maintain certain standards. Your nature
is all you can know of mine. I'm not a tub
of saline slopping around the world, nor yet

'the infinitely pleated tunic of the god,' and certainly
no kind of bosom. Pay attention
and watch your language." "Thank you, sea," I say.
The sky is darkening and drops of rain

fly on the warm wind, making me feel Romantic,
alone with the sea. We only have ten minutes
till I go to dinner: when at last I turn away
sea and sky are black, invisible.

November 5, 2000

Solstice Song

You can sing about the rain
but it won't do a damn bit of good.
You might as well talk to the wall.
You might as well talk to the cat:

he'll purr and raise the flag of pleasure
showing you what kind of meaning
lives in a voice free of the need for words.
We know what tears are: how about a song

for arctic air spilling over the mountains
down the inlets and valleys to the sea
clearing the sky so holly berries blaze redder
and self-pity shrinks and freezes dry and hard

and crackles satisfactorily underfoot
and even in a day of just eight hours of light
spirit expands to fill the time allotted
and rain is white crystal under the fallen leaves?

December 12, 2000

Canoe Meditation

Recurring image — stuck slide or holy card:
like infant Moses in his floating casket
memory's child within the canoe's bent ribs,
grizzled guardians bow and stern,
water smooth, "black
as the devil's dinnerbag,"
bottomless, warm as blood ...

If you can read this you're too close.

Didn't some tumbling water
mumble a name, dissolve it in the river
dropping clear to the filthy harbour of no identity?
The water is losing its memory,
its useless mountain thoughts of falling snow,
the sound of falling snow the only sound.

Gratitude wells up for no reason,
sheer gratefulness of an animal
momentarily unthreatened, sparrows back-kicking
black seed husks, not a hawk to be seen —
enormous relief, the execution postponed.
Time fattens;
afternoons swell like apples.

Rebuilding weary networks,
eyes, athletes of perception
free from the grim drill of print
and built monotony, zoom through bush shadows like bats.

Lids droop closed
over the bone caves they home to
and blackness fills with nothing
but twin bellows, dumb blood thudding, the steady
high keening of nerve:

that's the world singing in you, no, humming
you, beating a rough time,

chanting the alphabet of birds
and moving water, intimate murmur
of world-conversation, world-nakedness.

April 13, 2001

As if You Knew

The window's open so the birds can hear
WJKS, Where Joy Killed Sorrow,
dopey loveworn twanging
accelerated into good humour

as if setting a life sentence to music
—"Let me out," even, or
"Drinking beer and working" —
was a solution, that you could dissolve

past and future, the walls around your life
into a liquid moment flowing
no further than you hear or see.
A crow scrapes green mould off a branch.

Its bitter taste. McReynolds picking
on guitar, clawhammer banjo, glad
clatter. That brief
freedom of the bush.

May 18, 2001

Two Heavens

Mountainous rearings-up and wearings-down,
your inner insect chorus chirping
defects of character, remissnesses ...
lyrical "I am"s from treetops giving voice

to "that oceanic feeling:"
you wish you were here
more often, were everywhere more aware
of feet pressing the ground, of lungs expanding, filling,

turning air into vision, blood pushing,
loaded with life and death.
What are you to do with this knowledge?
The forest pours into your eyes,

into the dark torrent behind them,
it pours in, uncontained. A fallen trunk
softens, a column of moss
relaxing into the earth.

June 7, 2001

Torso

How free it feels, to be unnecessary!
— ungod, one creature among others
living through disaster's anniversaries.
Gave up a good situation to survive:

you'd have been shrinking while your pension grew
and you were put to use like a parrot
pulling a little cart. Now you're employed
watching the tops of trees move as the wind

moves them. Your amateur observations
go unrecorded unless absorbed, transformed:
green lichen dusting a barky crevice
shaped to the cadence of one particular bird's

call, heard once, on one particular day.
Dozens of robin generations later
someone whistles a phrase, a line they read
somewhere, so love of the world's remembered.

June 15, 2001

I'll Fly Away

Asleep in summer heat does wildness dream
of biting through the bars into a world
without us, its nightmare?

Mercifully most of their life is free
of forethought: unpuzzled, the sensible animals
turn at once from bulldozers and dust
where generations rollicked with their babies.

Prodigal:
rain puddles rimmed with yellow pollen;
unceasing:
moss creeping upslope, softening scree;

go deep. Essential work
ignores so-called civilization
and the future, as it forms them: finds a voice
below words, where the songs come from.

June 25, 2001

With My Head on Upside Down

The river's plump today,
sister I never had, always leaving —
why tot up a life's balance of feelings
valid only on the day of issue?

If I just lie on the couch all day
wrapped in my mum's old afghan
and watch the rain slip off the shining leaves,
soaking the earth, bound for the open ocean,

I miss you terribly.
You well up
through the fractured boilerplate — remember the time
Scamp got porcupined, and we gave him half a Valium

before we pulled the quills with a pair of pliers
and he got staggery and fell down the stairs?
— Oh, no, you weren't there.
There's not a day goes by that I don't think of you.

October 21, 2001

Nostalgia

All the old signs are gone, their flaking paint —
TIME IS SHORT, ETERNITY WHERE? on a barn —
everything's new now.
You've got to hand it to them.

We used to spend the whole day doing nothing
useful.
We'd poke around under the bridge
before anybody was up.

The empty street.
A man with red ribbons in his white beard
tramped through with two friendly young Huskies.
How I wanted to go with those dogs!

To tell the truth, I was alone, and lonely.
That must have been fifty years ago.
The old man is dead,
and the dogs are dead.

November 15, 2001

Scavenger

Not sure what I'm worth — something, anyway.
There's love and work
and I know how to work.
What's thrown out drives a rickety kind of economy

on rusting shopping carts. Down city lanes
not yet totally asphalt, amaranth
and other weeds ("a plant whose virtues
have not yet been discovered")

make things more homey, more human somehow.
But that's just me.
Jesus, the wrecks outside the Army and Navy —
Pat, how've you been? — face grey, hollowing, going ...

Hopped up, he bent my ear with his big projects.
Under the SkyTrain Millennium Line a drainpipe's trickle
feeds an ochre puddle and its clouds of miso — algae!
Its blue skin, oil-like, clinging in sheets, alive.

December 11, 2001

Written in the Dark

Swerving, avoiding pleasure for a plod
through literary canon theory, signifies nothing
good for reputation.
Dying helps.

A sharp-shinned hawk strafes a black squirrel under a car,
is driven off. Starving. Furious.
Wild in the city, egg-stealers
devour variety to feed the mob.

As sparrow fringes, jumpy, map the fan-
shaped killing range of dozing cats, forest
borders shrink from cities, scenting extinction.
Poor Canada. These boots will see me out.

The perception of the external world
by the senses, aesthesis, our anchor,
catapults us into sanity
despite our every effort to escape.

March 29, 2002

Snapper

Everything stops. If only.
As you jolt along in the executioner's cart
you're like one under the mud, you say nothing.
Mossback, you've watched so many daylights fade

to hope alone.
I wish I knew your thoughts.
You have no responsibility for how you've been injured.
You carry your own bags.

My good friends almost murdered,
your eggs laid in sand banks looted,
round white shells broken open, gobbled, dropped.
Why so comfortable with catastrophe?

Not mine. Not mine yet.
However long the darkness
it holds the music of what loves to happen,
insistent, indestructible, inhuman.

June 14, 2002

Wiggisey

Beavers make a warm home out of mud and sticks,
all the best materials, neurochemical events
will wind and bind us through the years,
we'll have work every day.

Feed, little perch, on blurry water surface,
troll the aisles of your insect supermarket.
I'm sorry for your trouble, Failure To Thrive,
and tell your mother I said so if you see her.

I leaned on the rail, left hand in a pool of water,
and felt neither yea nor nay, in paradise,
"living where choice and decision didn't enter,"
outside the domain of the will, if not of time.

If no one is shooting at you;
if no one is threatening you with torture;
if no one is bulldozing your home:
you can appreciate the hummingbird's pendulum dance.

June 18, 2002

Loonling

for Rachel Saunders, 1984-2006

CBC Radio Brave New Waves turns crepitus to music
and closer home old bones go elemental
after long delicious complication.
Rain, hot tears, purge the poison

of unfeeling. Our griefs celebrate
life in brief, homecoming and leaving,
where every gain is loss and change is death.
Soon enough our instruments of joy

will swell at best only as far as pleasure
(as if that weren't enough),
as if a group of players lost their strength
and numbers till the music only played

in the mind, that silent violin
whose body is all air, all living woods,
all lakes unknowing what their darkness holds,
all children ill, all their parents awake.

July 3, 2002

Bank Beaver

Long in the tooth, hard to get along with —
get out of the house.
"Pore old fella."
Farewell to desire for desire.

It diminishes over shallow lilied water
into the forest, feet wet on the shore.
Who knew you'd have all the world you wanted?
This time of last things you've been ready for

since you began, so many years ago,
is merely one layer, one stain of age
on the venerable monument of your life,
orange lichen on rock, the scour of ice,

the bay brim-full with your imagination,
what the wind scribbled on you, trails of rain,
how lucky you felt to see the water snake
swim close, how it knew how to disappear.

July 9, 2002

An Economics of Happiness

I'll see your mistake, and double it.
Orange King Billy, Our Guide to the Open Bible,
proclaims, "It's just a text," but we suspect
plant scents, or cloud ripples on ponds

are irreducible, pointing at nothing
but themselves, our efforts to capture them
bright innocent chalk smears on slate,
unwitting self-portraits

made for praise, half-consciously, the food
we need to grow into our loneliness.
Ghost children soothe, and settle, seeing a smile
even though they know they'll always be invisible.

White lilies have passed, yellow come on.
Soon all will be pillowed with snow.
The frogs don't know.
"Donk," they say. A mother drinks, and her fawn.

July 24, 2002

Inenarrable

Is it too much to ask, to ask the mind's
silence, for just one fucking minute?
Fifteen breaths. Green amphibian calm.
Splash of something taken, something murdered.

The flowing air feels cool inside your head,
your open throat. Some part of you is wise
to years, how seasons accelerate:
blackflies, sandflies, horseflies, deerflies, snow flies.

August leaves rattle, hectic with death.
Wake up and smell the formaldehyde,
chloroform porridge. Because you have to die
pale green rock moss is a paler green;

pitiless, the hawk's savage life
seems pitifully short. Crouched in my chest
are sobs, hunchbacked breath-hogs afraid of letting life
slip away like air.

November 28, 2002

Person of Snow

Tom Thomson couldn't draw people for beans
but that doesn't stop us loving those
holy glows, deep in the bottom galleries,
a conflagolion of Canadian

identities.
There's just so much to say and then you're dead.
"So what happened."
"Oh, a guy had a seizure."

"I'm goin' to stupid school. The teacher came in
and played for us on the guitar and the mandolin."
"I've moved up from Elmer's and Lepage's:
I'm on prescription glue."

I hope it helped. I know my parents
did the best they could. Here we are, aren't we.
Hear me out or not, it's your birthday.
I've got a secret. You.

March 23, 2003

War Baby

"Nobody helped me." "Something big and metal
is moving." Snug as a snail in its flak jacket
brooding over entropy, O deathy death
I'm tired of pulling you around in the wagon.

In all natural history's grand assembly
and dispersal, you're the one event the vultures watch for
but that's their business. You begin
where understanding ends, so a sound mind

turns gratefully back from your abstraction
to plunge into its own wealth of world-awareness,
like Scrooge McDuck in his coin-filled swimming pool.
We revel in having more than we deserve,

more than can ever be taken away
however rapidly decimated, some scrubby bush
to wander in, or just wind spinning some paper
unexpectedly before hurrying on.

May 21, 2003

Post-Industrial Landscape

Once in it I choose bewilderment
till reason is overthrown and I imagine
the wild deer's wet muzzle in my palm.
Now I understand the shadow message

leaves stammer on rock, the useless language
the sun taught me before I fell asleep
and woke up talking. Tiny furnaces
of decay sing immortality

into the soil, from whence springs all delight
and all terror. My gaze fastens with relief
on a green-skinned caterpillar, as if its beauty
led to an explanation. There are none

that would not insult a consciousness
they could contain. For some they ease the panic
of walls falling, self-forgetfulness.
Description helps; or counting breaths: One. One.

June 17, 2003

Bedford Social

Firewood's sixty-five dollars a cord:
but these woods and I work only for ourselves
and each other, though it's hard to see
what good I do it, aside from letting it be.

In rippling water a tube of grey mesh flexes:
a cast-off snake skin. The jaws open and close.
High on young wings, a raven yawps —
maybe the one we rescued, cooped in a crevice,

too stooped to fly, the rock stained with days of droppings,
the bird weakening, starving, stuck. How *real* it felt,
rowing him to safe haven, perched on a paddle blade,
his smart, bright eye on us: "A rich, full life ..."

You, reader, must be wondering,
"How do the woods work for him?" Think of the raven
transported out of hell, by what might kill him
but acts like love. Trust? I'm safe so far.

July 3, 2003

Empire

Almost desolating, this distance I feel
between myself and the "rather immature
forest" I want so much to be a part of,
though in what sense, even as it surrounds me,

could that be true, aside from the molecular
shapes I share with muskrat or white pine,
those wholly imperceptible elemental
structures, whizzing zones of mathematical

uncertainty? In a better mood
I seem to share the spirit of the place
— fuzzier even than electron clouds —
and that must be enough. My clinging mind

can coat whole galaxies with its shiny trail
for the infant comfort of its own reflection.
All that's out there, unknowing and unknown,
that is my face before I was born.

July 13, 2003

Wetland

"Potato chip, potato chip," goldfinches
lilt over the beaver dam, "just givin' 'er;"
downstream the little waterfall
pours loveliness unstintingly:

sulfur-brilliant, whitely falling saviours.
Leopard frog, happy and rich like me
on the muddy margins, your perfect
meditation soothes this venomous mood,

forgives my bloody boyhood ignorant
as dirt, stoning your kin.
                          May money and law
serve and protect our vulnerable cathedral

flimsy as chain fern leaf or dragonfly
wing, dear as our spouse's body loved
lifelong, freely giving, deepening us
out of our tiny knowing.

September 3, 2003

Indian Summer

Year follows year, meadowhawk dragonflies
dry new wings, black-veined, wrinkled windows.
What we think we know is the same straitjacket,
what we lack the same lack,

all the time in the world.
Leaves turn to brilliant going-away
presents: envious, I'd love to learn
festive, spectacular good-byes

to the visible remembered world,
more than resigned, considerately cheering
the living with incandescent memento
mori, mimicking exemplary

loving humans, as well as other creatures
oblivious of me as cloud formations:
fast, strong fliers, fall's last
butterflies, Mourning Cloak, Question Mark.

October 21, 2003

Catbirds, Mockingbirds, Starlings

Birds repeat their parents' songs
as if their lives depend on it.
They do:
catbirds, mockingbirds, starlings

mimic birds or fire alarms but sound
like catbirds, mockingbirds, starlings.
I compare my tongue-tied goodbye:
"You're dying, Mum."

Stupid: I only hope
she was unconscious. (Was there a hand-squeeze?
Sometimes I tailor comfortless memories.)
I spoke so she'd know I was there, that's all.

Her chest sank on each useless breath:
her lungs were full of fluid. She was drowning.
Pneumonia, the friend of suffering.
Unthinking, comfortless: at last, a truth we knew.

July 23, 2004

Devil's Paintbrush

In my slow-burning archive orange hawkweed
thrives in granite-charactered soil
spalled off the basement stone,
a beaver labours up her steep skid road

logging poplar for food and shelter,
wind drives rivers of ripples down a pond.
Everything here knows what to do.
Like a bogus boiler inspector

I investigate every valve, work and rework
notes to husks, skeletal remains,
survivors who revive experience.
I try to memorize, to make some pictures

to walk into, in the final time
when I can't walk or hear or see, and see
lake-cradling pink granite, its orange earth,
its skin of lives flickering, flickering.

August 22, 2004

In Loco Parentis

No easy way: the fabric of non-life
crumbles into smallness like sandstone
or plastic — broken-down bits everywhere,
scientists say, in tiny creatures, big:

accidental, inert, unusable.
Our animal death will be different:
cannibalizable, we will survive
in our survivors: a face less

and less clear, a voice fading
to silence; may have taught someone
to read or write, or sing a cheerful song
passed on; showed an uncomplaining

face to pain a friend took courage from.
Or we may merely have added one
way to look at water moving, one
delay against disorder: living wants complication.

September 22, 2004

The Elgin Angular Unconformity

The bay's inviting, sunny ripple lines
waver over the sand, but it's too cold
to swim. The bank beaver, impervious,
plows around the point like a dreadnought

securing a perimeter. A teacup-
sized snapping turtle pokes her chisel nose
up into the cooling air.
Most birds have gone: insect trills,

wind in leaves, faint calls of southbound geese,
the high, almost unnoticeably growing
ringing in your head … this last
the surest sign of a winter coming

from which there is no flying.
I am not much comforted that one life stops
to continue a while, somehow, in others.
I take off my shoes and socks and wade in the cold water.

September 30, 2004

The Secret of What Is Important

The work of love's a good kind of order
to scare yourself into: any excuse
can pull you in the ditch and leach your bones
until the clouds lose patience and race on.

Clouds favour people without your fancy problems,
just city people who pay their kid's fare with a joke:
"Now don't go shootin' any more people on the bus:
I gave you that gun for a purpose."

She loves you,
goes the old song, and I know that's true
sometimes. Sometimes I feel so tired
the fight to keep on the surface of the earth

is barely worth it. One day I'll just let go
in maybe a hundred years if no one's around
who minds too much and life is pain all day
and the world and I don't care for each other at all.

May 12, 2005

Galactic Dynamics

So long as inertia's great flywheel holds all in place
why complain about the weather? Let it teach us
to vary, repeat ourselves, defy prediction.
At least we're here. "Cheer," calls the red-winged blackbird.

That call and one song are all it needs.
A better example might be the selfless moon
who climbs and sinks over the night-charmed earth,
horizons separating, entering each other.

Selves, bodies, wisdoms working together, wet
with complexity, weak and strong forces
constellated in us, what do you say?
Never stop

is all we know. One law
grinds our bones, another licks our pleasure
until it swells and flowers
into the future. Love what you have.

May 31, 2005

Stable Base

Two blue dragonflies stuck together fly
head to tail like two B-52s
refuelling, robot insect energy
driving too our poor pure animal brains

locked in human cells, clocks overwound
against the awful fact of all our endings,
generations swept away, firefly
pale green flashes weak against black, gone.

Rock, rock. The lake's small waves lapping.
A Tiger Swallowtail feasts on black dung
dropped by some small animal,
shiny with seed or insect hulls.

Wings slowly fanning, it seems to revel in
life driven only by animal insect energy,
glad in its brief time, seems to dying say
to onrushing death, So fucking what.

July 22, 2005

Garter Lake Gazette

Now we've found how fast electrons
hop from atom to atom — something, quintillionths …
In our '86 Olds
we amble the rocky lane, frog juggernaut,

soaring any road like bird or angel.
This car life can't survive
Alberta light sweet crude at $100 a barrel:
"demand destruction." Cauliflower-brained

cumulus congestus boils and swells
up to the stratosphere and turns to ice
eight miles above its trail of rain and thunder
missing our parching forest. Some southern

dryland opportunists will thrive here
in future weather, some Neo-Neolithic
dragonflyherd tending glittering wings
will read this and understand perfectly.

August 25, 2005

Babies' Cottage

Where do we come from?
What are we?
Where are we going?
Don't ask.

The mountains across the harbour
were a chain of offshore islands
before their long slow crash
into British Columbia.

The ground we walk on, hard-packed clay and gravel,
was carried down the mountains
by glaciers and rivers now vanished.
The hospice around the corner

once housed family court;
before that it was Babies' Cottage, an orphanage.
Someone sits by a lamp in the fog-shrouded lounge.
Above the fog, we are told, the sun is shining.

November 23, 2005

Mother's Day

Dear Nature,
I'm sorry I haven't written
more often. I'm full of excuses — work avoidance
may be a high-sounding name for laziness

but hints at the terror of never being good
enough, hiding, one of those
"inadequates" they used to
put down like sickly kittens.

                      Infant fears,
exaggerated shadows — let's forget them:
it's your day. Overcast; the southeast wind
scatters wild cherry petals,

star-patterning the path. Thanks for that.
Grey Precambrian ribs gleam in the rain,
lichen bloom mottles the glacier scars,
mosses, grasses fur levels and crevices.

May 14, 2006

Lily Pond Margin

Not much happening: the slack-string
calls of green frogs barely keep
the conversation (if it is
a conversation, thick with pause

or overlapping) alive;
twenty-two black and shining
turtles clamber onto half-sunk logs;
while I watch them dry

scuffed-shoe colour,
a fawn teeters gingerly away
from its bed practically
under my nose, to lie somewhere

else invisible;
south of here, the TSX
consolidates after resource profit-taking,
strengthens to ten, six at the close.

June 18, 2006

Rivers and Mountains

High haze: a ring around the sun:
bright overcast: hand's shadow
fades on the page: clouds
tow blue sky on warm wind.

Human busyness
is a wasp's buzz in the forest.
Pensioners, short-term contractors,
content, we can afford to let trees fall

unharvested, to feed the wilderness.
Up in the hardwood canopy
a wood thrush out-lieders rivals to persuade
an open-hearted listener it's all good.

Breezes brush the bay, sky-coloured
ripples advance, waver, reverse, we
follow somehow, shimmer, transient,
far sun-flicker stammering.

July 27, 2006

Minnows

So … unlikely: so many feet above
the lake, in ponds filled with nothing but rain
minnows are springing half a finger length
out of the water, little Gothic windows

flashing and sinking back into rings of ripples.
How did they get here? — How did any of us?
A biologist friend explains they must have climbed
the tiny streams whose dry black beds run inches deep

in spring and fall; or birds may have dropped them —
poetic beginnings, romantic but scientific.
Until she said they'd be there I never saw them.
What else lives in here? A lifetime couldn't count them all

yet once there wasn't a single living thing
on earth: chemicals, complex mixes, lightning, and
something began remaking itself, stubborn,
creeping like happiness across the landscape.

October 5, 2006

Notes on the poems

"Bushed:"

Stanley Howard Knowles, 1908-1997. M.P. 1942-58, 1962-84; Officer of the Order of Canada; honorary officer of the House of Commons for life; he used his legendary knowledge of parliamentary procedure to promote social justice and enlarge Canada's welfare state.

Mountain flour consists of fine particles of limestone eroded from the Rocky Mountains. Suspended in the lakes of the region, it gives them their characteristic green colour.

Bow Falls is on the Bow River near Banff, Alberta.

"Columbine:"

Stephen Reid is the author of a novel, *Jackrabbit Parole*, and the subject of *The Stopwatch Gang*, an account of a gang of bank robbers. He is married to the poet Susan Musgrave.

"Across The Line:"

The English transcription of the bird's call is from *Birds of Ontario*, by Andy Bezener (Lone Pine, 2000.)

Elizabeth MacCallum, the granddaughter of Tom Thomson's patron, and John Fraser own a cottage on Split Rock Island on Georgian Bay, in West Muskoka, where this poem was written.

"Noise:"

"Spudger" is an English colloquialism for sparrow.

"Diary:"

"Slipping glimpses" is a phrase of Willem de Kooning's.

"Pink:"

"A corporation" is slang for "a prominent belly."

"Fountain:"

The first line refers to the last line of Rilke's "Antique Torso of Apollo:" "Du musst dein Leben andern" — "You must change your life." Ken Snyder saw this on a bumper sticker in Berkeley, California in the sixties.

"Here:"

"some bush to look out on:" from an interview with the Nova Scotia artist Maud Lewis (1903-1970). Severely handicapped by poverty, birth defects, and arthritis, she dedicated her life to her art to give us an idyllic vision of rural Nova Scotia.

"Influence:"

"Stupid as a painter" was a 19th century Parisian insult.

Adding 39 to the number of cricket chirps in 15 seconds gives the temperature in degrees Fahrenheit.

"As if You Knew:"

Line two is from an interview with Bill Munroe, the great bluegrass artist.

McReynolds picking is a guitar playing technique.

Honoured visitors to aboriginal lands in Australia were offered the freedom of the bush, equivalent to the keys to the city.

"Torso:"

Line 11 replicates the rhythm of one robin's call heard in Banff, June 2001.

"I'll Fly Away:"

The title is the title of a gospel song by Alfred E. Brumley.

"With My Head on Upside Down:"

Line six: written during the American invasion of Afghanistan, 2001. An afghan is a type of heavy coverlet.

"Nostalgia:"

The sign was painted on a barn at the Locks, on the North Muskoka River near Huntsville.

"Scavenger:"

Weeds of Canada attributes the quote about weeds to Ralph Waldo Emerson.

Freud considered love and work the only salvation for the human condition.

"Wiggisey:"

The title is perhaps an Algonquin or Ojibway word for house. My father often used it, as in, "Do you find it cold in this wiggisey, Ethel?"

"Loonling:"

"Crepitus" is a medical term for the sound made by creaking joints. CBC 2 broadcast a musical performance incorporating these sounds.

Tears are a means of excreting toxins from the body.

"Bank Beaver:"

Bank beavers are older males who have been expelled from the lodge and make their home in a river or lake bank.

"An Economics of Happiness:"

The Orange Order, a Protestant fraternal society, was founded in 1759 in Ireland to commemorate the victory of William of Orange at the Battle of the Boyne in 1690. The quoted phrase appears on banners carried in the annual Orange Parade on July 12, the Protestant equivalent of Saint Patrick's Day.

"Person of Snow:"

The quotes in this poem were overheard on the #4 Powell bus in east Vancouver.

"Conflagolion" is an Ottawa Valley word for a confusing tangle, a snarl, a maze.

"Inenarrable:"

Chlorinated tap water, when heated, reacts with naturally occurring organic compounds to form formaldehyde and chloroform gases.

"War Baby:"

The second quote is from a US military spokesperson during the American invasion of Iraq, 2003.

"Empire:"

"What was your face before you were born?" is a Zen koan, a form of paradoxical question used to direct the mind toward enlightenment, or right understanding.

"Wetland:"

The goldfinch's call is from *Birds of Ontario*.

"[M]oney and law" refers to nature conservancies' programs of helping landowners maintain natural heritage in perpetuity.

Acknowledgements

I am grateful to the Canada Council for the Arts, the Ontario Arts Council, and The Banff Centre for the Arts for financial support during the writing of this book, to Judith Fitzgerald, Al Moritz, Ken Snyder, and Miriam Clavir for their valuable suggestions, and to Elizabeth Philips for her generous editing for the press.

Some of these poems first appeared in *The Antigonish Review*, *Canadian Literature*, *The Capilano Review*, the CBC's *Choral Concert*, *Event*, *The Fiddlehead*, *Grain*, *The Malahat Review*, *Perihelion*, *Prairie Fire*, *Rampike*, and the anthology *Why I Sing the Blues* (Vancouver; Smoking Lung Press, 2001).

A native of Baysville, in Ontario's Muskoka region, John Donlan is a poetry editor with Brick Books. He spends half the year as a reference librarian at the Vancouver Public Library, and the other half writing poetry near Godfrey, Ontario. His collections of poetry are *Domestic Economy* (Brick Books, 1990, reprinted 1997), *Baysville* (House of Anansi Press, 1993) and *Green Man* (Ronsdale Press, 1999). He is also the author of *A Guide to Research @ Your Library* (Ontario Library Association/Vancouver Public Library, 2002).